I0134215

Somehow We Remain in the Aftermath

poems by

Sara Krueger

Finishing Line Press
Georgetown, Kentucky

Somehow We Remain in the Aftermath

ACKNOWLEDGMENTS

The poems Mama Said, Becoming Robot, and Metal Moonrise were first
published in the Fall 2014 issue of *Menacing Hedge*.
The poem Hunger was first published in Issue 64 of *Jersey Devil Press*.
The poem Sun Lamps was first published in Volume Two: Issue Two of
Driftwood Press.
The poem Surfacing was first published in Issue 12 of *Devilfish Review*.

Publisher: Leah Maines

Editor: Christen Kincaid

Cover Art: Quinton Baker

Author Photo: Samantha Sanchez

Cover Design: Elizabeth Maines

Printed in the USA on acid-free paper.
Order online: www.finishinglinepress.com
        also available on amazon.com

Author inquiries and mail orders:
Finishing Line Press
P. O. Box 1626
Georgetown, Kentucky 40324
USA

Table of Contents

To David Heckler, a warrior writer that nourishes my soul. Preethy Vallala, my mystic and guide to the absurd. Samantha Sanchez, for her gentle encouragement and creative insights. Francine Sanders, for having duende and embracing the senses. Jillian Axtell, for her generous heart and open mind. Jessica Mitton, for her fearless spirit and boundless optimism. Susan Spillers, for bringing me into this world and believing in me with unmatched intensity.

And, to Garrett, for always being.

STORY KEEPERS

We are the Story Keepers.

In our collections
we tell of the times before
and the times since.
Of what they want to know
and what they'd rather not.

Spines crack and fray
from floor to ceiling
through each and every vault.
And we spend the years
fixing and fidgeting
and playing games of sneak and snatch.

And once in a great while,
when the light is waning
and boredom beats about us,
we choose someone
from the shelves
and open our ears.

MAMA SAID

Mama said my birth was all regret.
Said she'd rather end the line herself than some company.
But, bodies let you down.

Right before her clock stilled,
Mama squinted at the sparrows
plummeting in twos and threes from the rusted-out sky,
and she said not to turn silver.
Said I'd get more pleasure being the color of apricots.

It was hard to believe such things
when her own bruised fruit tremored with the sick,
just a few suspended seconds of spit and spray,
before her hand dropped away from mine.

I stayed close to the trees Mama planted
like she said to do.
Thumbed the thick ooze of yellow rain beaded on glass
and breathed in their fading green.
Still, I knew.
And she knew.
The withering would take them too.

Mama said it'd be hard to stop
the putting of pen to paper.
Said hope was as close to sinning as you could get.
Mama said and she said and her words were pregnant
with a quaking truth.

Flesh is a sin too.
That's what they said.
And I was one of the last sinners.
Feeling the feelings.
As many feelings as a body can stand
before it lets you down.

BECOMING ROBOT

Straining nostrils
that pioneer outward,
gatherers of last breaths.

And there it is blooming.
Sweet smell of rotting sick
like pineapple syrup from a can,
with an undertone of aluminum—
a flavor note
appearing right when the brochure said it would.

Electrodes make the skin jump,
signaling I'm still alive
for four more days by their estimate.

Eyes skitter left and right,
tracking shoes bone-white and always moving
above my hydro tank
where I rest on the surface
like a water strider.

It is too hard to keep this pace.
I let the soft sucking sounds of the tubes lull me,
dropping as they do
to wriggle along this ruined body,
basting it in a little more mercury.

I tell myself,
never mind these cracked, bleeding lips
and burning throat.
They will vanish in the last stage of transformation
when all becomes metal,
from toes to tummy to tongue,
and I end the line.

METAL MOONRISE

Now I walk with the fireflies,
fluid the very same neon
slowly pumping to all my parts.
Moonshine is all my metal can manage—
a detail left for the fine print.

I scrape and squeak through the browning reeds,
a few steps behind the others,
on our nightly pilgrimage to the company men.

In their white jumpsuits and elephantine masks,
they toil in the old factories.
Hoses tossed over shoulders like ties at long ago meals,
they fix us up so we can continue
in our clean-up crews stretching the waterways.
Praying for a day when the lines will start again.

And I wonder about this second chance they sold
as the crabs click clack like cutlery against me.
I wonder what I am now and what I ever was.
After all there is no heart, no skin to touch.
Only viscous liquid,
cog wheels and springs,
and hammered steel plating.

Mama said I'd turn and turn
until recognition failed.
Said she'd never know me
when she sat perched and peeking
from the big beyond.

And I wonder what I will ever be now,
laboring like this at a drowning depth
in the backwater bayous.
Paying the payment I signed for
when I left my flesh behind.

STORY SEEKERS

We are the Story Seekers.

With wishes brimming
behind the eyes they gave us:

To have the company men visit
more often than they do.
To have them rest in our corridors
and feel us
with ungloved hands.

To know the ones too
that move on their own
along the rivers
and between the trees.

Oh, to meet someone, anyone new,
and learn them.
To hear a knocking
and see hands wrap around
the wooden doors of this place
and push.

To fill our shelves
with stories simple and strange.
To fill and fill
until they spill everywhere
and we have as many reasons to tend them.

COMPANY MAN

Another wretched night comes,
with the cleaners trudging
line after line
towards my station.

We are a broken business—
a failed population
better suited to the halls of extinction.

We knew this.

Yet, we refused,
in all our limbic wisdom,
to let go gracefully.

Instead,
we burrowed,
borrowed,
and bargained.
And our sweet, sweet blue
kept on its way to becoming Venus.

Some of us cowered.
Others became lost.
Or we bent to the task,
driven by the hypnotic droning of the machines.
We even shucked our skins entirely
and slipped beneath the waters.

But somehow we remained in the aftermath,
like scattered husks
found after a hard harvest.

I arrange my tools
and get to it,
hating how many friends I see
in these faces I fix.

HUNGER

I float the back channels in the swampish heat,
past the leavings of one town and then another,
keeping my peepers peeled and my mask tugged tight.

Every few miles I shore up and scan the trees,
fingering the blade I rescued
from Gummy's hog farm.
My work boots sink into the muck
as I root around for something squirrely.

The search is so much harder now after the change.
But, Gummy needs the meat—
bloody and almost beating.
Her book tells us these things.

She'd got no teeth left in her head,
Gummy didn't,
when I found her.
Her eyes had gone too from many months of basement living.
She keeps me at this life now,
Gummy does,
and she makes me fancy
that it ain't just the metal men out there
rustling along in the dark.

KNOCKING

Today, I fill my lungs up
with the smell of real sea
for the first time in years,
and the salt burns my tongue.

I remember visiting the whirly top rides here
when I was little
and Papa still had his whiskers.
I remember the times before
when there were still people to see
and things to do.

The mountain waters
trickle into the sea
and I can't stop thinking of Papa
and his last days.

Three sunsets pass
with me sleeping
on the hard-packed sand
before I make my move,
avoiding the stone tunnels
like Papa warned.

I reach the city,
sprouting up in columns,
rising exclamations of what was.
I run a rubbered hand
along a welted metal girder
and I can almost hear them
from the burnt-out shop windows.

Condensation fogs my glass vision panel.
No more time.
I stumble through the streets,
empty as they are,
an infinite number of trajectories.

Finally I see them,
the domes of the diversion galleries
glowing through the day's haze.
If only Papa could know I made it.

I reach the barricaded doors
and knock
and knock
and knock again.

Faint bruises puffing up
on my palms
as I hear something shift inside.

STORY TELLERS

We are the Story Tellers.

Spinning yarns,
and tall tales too,
with digital banjo pickings
and firelight
tumbling from our barrel chests.

Programmed to sustain the ones
that turned like tides,
seeping into the ground.

We wait and wait,
but they never come back.

From time to time
you can hear them
through the sewer grates,
or so the cleaners say.
Just whispering wisps
and wavering shadows.

We try to bet at
when they'll breed and birth.
When they might be ready to remember
and crawl out of their hidey-holes—
own what we've protected.

When they will decide
to shut down the controls
and release us
to where the nights are forever.

ARRIVAL

I am the first to feel the pain
after abandoning the above
for permanent night and candle stars.

Wiping away nine months of warmth and wet,
I cradle this new one
to breasts desert dry
and worry on the few powders that we found
tucked amongst our stores.

With a shaking hand,
I shoo away the others that crouch and sway
along this shattered vessel of mine.

Laying him out on the cool earth,
I behold his tiny fists
as they find purchase in this weakened world.
I press clumps of radiated soil between my palms,
releasing them to break along his belly,
and think of all the goodbyes beyond number.

I think of dad in his plaids
and how his dust swirls and settles now
in never-ending sand storms.
Think of how he is tamped down
by animal paws—
bubbled pink and shiny.

The hurt arrives with a deep heat again,
body sweat-soaked and seizing
as the last of it exits.

His feeble bleating sears through me
and I can't look anymore,
knowing what they have in store.

I leave him squirming worm-like in the dim,
to stumble along tunnels
built years before the sky turned.

Trailing my fingers along the aging pipework,
I tell and tell myself
how I should be glad for him
and the days coming
when so many chose to end their lines.

SUN LAMPS

Down Subway Tunnel A
we go
to the City Center,
our heads ducked in reverence.

Reaching the sun lamps
that loom in the dank,
I deposit my blanket bundle dutifully
before we hop quick-footed across the tracks
to safely tuck along the limestone walls
in one snaking chain.

From the shadows we watch
behind ground glass goggles
as dials are cranked from level one to two to three
by the twitchy hands of scientists
schooled by dog-eared consumer manuals.

They pace and postulate,
these hopeful men in their rubber sun suits,
until the timers tick, tick, ding
and the white coats appear
to flip this baby of mine from back to belly.

Little chicken crisping.
He goos and gaas in his box,
sporting onion-thin skin
that will soon blister and blossom into
a hundred raw rosettes.

I record his progress
in a baby book rescued from the Other Times.
Dreaming dreams like any parent might—
of pulling plugs on the cleaners that move in the moonlight.

SURFACING

Today,
the bulbous silver heads of the cleaners
snapped back to the sky.

When they fell,
they sent along such a rumbling
like no one had ever heard—
the sound of making space
for beginnings.

We had all hoped for a sun-drunk brood.
But there is only the one I delivered.
Him—
with a skin so scaly thick,
rolling mud balls like a little dung beetle.

I shepherd him halfheartedly
as his chubby legs scoot along the tunnels,
imagining what he will find
and what he won't,
and I realize he will likely not care.

Before we sever ties,
I scoop him up to say my piece,
to impart some small insight
that will rattle around his memories.

But, I am only able to mumble
about the time I went to a drive-in with a boy
and flinched at the skull-crushing mandibles
of 50-foot-tall ants.
How that boy's hands felt
and how his lips were salty sweet with kettle corn.

The others wrestle him from my arms
and unlock the subway gates,
placing him gently on the tiles
so he can climb the exit stairs.

I hear the pattering of rain
coming from above
and suppose I am happy he will taste it.

The others surround me
so I can no longer see.

A chorus of voices erupt—
He will go it alone like we taught him.
He will be more than fine.
He will be able to stand the dusks and the dawns,
just think of it,
and if he's lucky, maybe more.

Maybe he will swim in the sea
or even find a girl out there
and feel those first fires.
Yes, yes,
a girl
and he will fill her womb.

Such small consolations they name,
hanging thin in the air.

I shove through the circle
of white coats and scientists.
Push past the worn-out men
and the would-be baby makers too.

I run from them all,
already longing for a day
when his feet cross the subway vents
above me
and give a glimpse
of what he has become.

STORY MAKERS

We are the Story Makers.

Each day we press ourselves to the windows,
searching for words
to record his story.

This new one—
he unfolds brown as a berry
through our telescopes
and runs along rock candy-colored beaches.

We get out our instruments
and carve his each and every moment.

He lazes about some days,
and others
he cartwheels.
Gets bolder.
Makes a game of dodging
the glinting bodies of the cleaners
that burn
in the high heat.

See how his tattered gauzes,
and eventually his mask,
rip away in the wind.
See him getting closer to our domes
as the days pass.

We record this too
and move to sit by the doors,
rocking and ready,
to christen him
with a warm smack into knowing.

Sara Krueger spent her early years in Michigan farm country sneaking tractor rides and cozying up with books by a potbelly stove. She owes much of her artistic sensibilities to her late uncle, who introduced her impressionable 6-year-old mind to David Lynch, Dr. Demento, German Expressionism, and 70's science fiction films. Her drive to write is fueled by memories of her late grandmother, who started playing with words in her 60's, proving that age should never defeat a dream.

Sara's work is brimming with charismatic woodland monsters, world-weary robots, doomed circus performers, and beings from other dimensions, all of who yearn for understanding and connection, but seldom find it. When she isn't writing, Sara enjoys walking the shores of Lake Michigan, making elaborate meals and music mixes for friends, and hunting for her next piece of taxidermy jewelry. Her stories and poems are available at: www.sara-krueger.com.

9 781944 899608